DAILY SELF-MANAGEMENT FOR ALL

ABDULRAHEEM KHAN

ISBN 979-888555651-4

Dedicated to my Mother

Contents

CHAPTER ONE

ANGER MANAGEMENT AT THE WORKPLACE: HOW TO DEAL WITH THE VIOLENCE AT THE WORKPLACE

Have you ever had that sort of meeting where a colleague lost his temper or just went on an unexpected crazy rant failing to deal with themselves under pressure? With most employers turning the heat to 100%, this has become relatively common in most professions where the demand is bound to crack even the toughest of stones.

Seeing a fellow employee undergo these fits of anger can have significant repercussions on the entire organisation, and you should understand their impact to learn how to handle them.

You might see employees dodging these people to avoid uncomfortable incidents, but this shouldn't be the case. There is a fine line between expressing yourself strongly and downright exploding on someone. This line should never be crossed as it might result in causing harm to someone and tarnishes the reputation of the entire company.

So, as employees, you should know how to deal with this anger, and you can avoid these incidents altogether. A few simple things you can do to be prepared to spring into action whenever needed are:

- ***Create a Professional Culture around you***

I'm sure most employees would prefer an office to have the professionalism not to allow belligerent employees to do whatever they want over offices that tolerate this behaviour. No one wants to come into work in a mud pit with savages blurting out whatever they see fit. This is also your responsibility as this kind of environment can only be hoped to be created if every employee communicates and professionally interacts with one another. They should also be trained on professional communication, negotiation and conflict resolution by the employer itself.

- ***Set expectations and always train your employees***

We can't expect every person in a company to have the same experiences and aspirations from how different our lifestyles are. This is why you must set expectations and demonstrate the behaviour we want them to have to train them how to communicate with each other even if the emotions get h

- ***Documenting the incidents properly***

When an associate or worker somehow acts in a way not suitable to the ethics and is suitably confronted about their behaviour, it is vital that the incident is documented correctly. Include documenting the date, time of the event, persons concerned and a short description of the situation that crystal rectified everything up to the incident. Add an outline of the incident and details of however it had been resolved. This history may well be necessary if there becomes a necessity to require further action or terminate the worker.

- ***Response Training***

Often staff don't have any idea how to deal with angry employees. They're caught off guard and struggle with what to mention or do. Teach them a way to communicate, respond, and what to try to do if they feel vulnerable or threatened.

Help them perceive when to speak up and when to contact the superior for help, they should also know the excellent they need to go to. This includes understanding the method to report an occasion so that matters can get resolved.

- ***Having a zero tolerance policy and adhering to it***

There ought to be no excuse and no exception for any worker that imparts a physical injury to a colleague.

An intolerance policy that's communicated through the worker orientation process and coaching permit you to quickly terminate the connection and take away the worker from the organisation. These are the legal powers you need to utilise to be swift when taking action, and you should consult an attorney to understand them completely.

Even with these precautions, there are other essential things to think about like:

- If staff don't feel safe at work, they're going to be distracted and in turn have lower productivity.
- When an associate worker acts out and isn't confronted, they're being sent a message that the behaviour is all right and is, therefore, more likely of repeating their actions
- Act on your gut instincts along with what you've been trained for when facing troublesome things.
- Intervention with associate anger management counsellor is usually useful for the morale of the workers and is, therefore, a grand prize to give up on.
- Decisions to terminate a belligerent worker are essential to apply and might even get especially troublesome as you may have a relationship with the employee.

Employees that come back should figure out the intention of doing what they have done and try to take special care to have a peaceful environment that's safe and free from hostility. It is usually the management's responsibility to make or break the culture of the entire office and to set the expectation for applicable interactions within the work. Our ignorance in the field of Mental Health is an essential and core flaw in our society. This outlook should be changed now, and employees should be taken care of mentally as well as physically.

CHAPTER TWO

WHAT IS THE IMPORTANCE OF BEING YOURSELF FIRST THAN ANYONE ELSE?

There are many people in a person's life where they think that they want to be like that person. Let it be according to their attitude, behaviour, their positivity or dedication to their work. Many people consider others as their idol and try to impersonate their way of doing things. This is most common among teens, college-going bunch and fresh out of college graduates who just entered the corporate world. Although the concept of idolising a person is always prevalent in everybody's life, it makes them forget about the fact that makes them stand out amongst themselves.

They are staying true to themselves.

Now there are way more benefits of being yourself in front of everybody. This makes people know what your strengths and weakness are and what you do and do not do and what makes you as a person happy and what doesn't make you happy. By being yourself, we can make sure that if the person is genuine or not. And moreover, at a workplace, the employer could give the employee who is true to themselves the kind of work which they can complete. Because if not, then it would be a scenario where the person is expected to some work which is not meant for them and could cause disappointment and stress.

The problem is that a person always keeps about thinking about how the society and the people around him would think about him. But they don't realise the fact that the community and the people around them would always judge them no matter what they do. And many of the people always act like they are someone not quite themselves. This leads to change. The person starts acting like they are someone else in the eyes of the people around them. But doing so would change the person's thought process and their way of pleasing others. Many people think that bot being themselves and faking it helps in impressing their boss, lover or even their colleagues. But by trying to impress them always makes the person look like a guy who is trying too hard. Forget about making a lasting impression, but they are quickly taken advantage of by their peer

The thing that the people don't get is that being themselves does not mean that the person is selfish and that they don't care about what others think. Being themselves is staying true to how you as a person are and doing what you feel like doing. It also means living your own life under your terms and not on somebody else's governance and thereby finding some self-love and respect for themselves. The person needs to know that society will continue to judge the person regardless of how they behave and what they do. So instead of listening and adjusting according to how the community wants the person to, the person could chuck it and live by their own rules.

Now there are many things which a person can learn by being themselves:

- **The person is not expected to be perfect:** No matter how right a person is, they are not always perfect. Perfection isn't something that can be achieved. And even if the person gives their 100 per cent into their work, then the genuine effort that they take would be the one who could help in gaining success.
- **The person can learn more about themselves and their surroundings:** Being themselves always has their perks. The person gets to know about themselves more and more every day, and sometimes, it continuously surprises them about discovering things about themselves. Knowing more about themselves helps in maintaining good relations with other people because the person knows how much the other person can tolerate.

- **This helps in setting goals:** People who stay true to themselves to consider their future goals and ambitions. This could help in being clear about their intentions beforehand. And also, this helps in maintaining focus over these goals that they have set for themselves.
- **The person is more confident in the choices that they opt:** No matter what happens, the person would only undertake the choices and decision based on their personal preference because the person would only know their limits and comfort through which they can work.
- **Staying true helps in maintaining your own identity:** For a person who is confident themselves who are those people who believe in their ideas, beliefs and their decision-making skills. And the person would get to know about the things they are passionate about. Which, in turn, helps them create their own identity.

The only thing left for a person is to believe in themselves and undertake every challenge by themselves and not try to imitate the lifestyle or things which others do.

CHAPTER THREE

BEING COMPARATIVE

It is a common observation that people often compare themselves to others who share similar attributes. Most self-help articles, books, and advice that you read will encourage you to stop comparing myself to others. You will see a famous tagline everywhere: To compare is to despair. True, many people make unreasonable comparisons to others who have achieved unusually high levels of success, thus causing them a great deal of pain and anxiety about their progress in life. However, these comparisons can sometimes be good measures of development. The comparison itself is not a problem at all. It is the train of thought that follows a comparison that can be harmful. Comparison can be used to crush and destroy your self-esteem to zero, and on the other hand, it can be used as a powerful tool for self-assessment and personal growth. While comparing yourself to somebody, ensure that you drag your mind along a positive line to gain maximum benefits from the comparison.

Benefits of Being Comparative

1. To compare is Inevitable.

Human beings are perceptive creatures, and we constantly observe and take note of our surroundings. Social comparison is wired into our very mind set. We cannot stop drawing analogies between one person and another and admittedly, the comparison is nothing to despair about. But it is that next thought that tags, along with the comparison, are problematic. It is the feeling of being inferior to somebody or feeling meagre concerning any aspect that bitters the idea of comparison. However, we can use a comparison to our advantage. A shift in our perspective is the only prerequisite to change our experience of life. Instead of complaining about the features that you lack concerning a person, evaluate your strengths. List the advantages that you have in comparison to the other person and rack your brain to find alternatives to make up for the lacking features.

2. To compare is to Research.

Instead of feeling envious of others or bad about yourself, consider researching on the features that someone else possesses over you. The more you notice what the people around you do, you become socially aware of yourself as well as your surroundings. Sometimes you may have an initial hit of envy, but then you can figure out if it is something that you want or not. If you have identified it as something that you want, you have already set the goals to work for, dreams to pursue and passions to follow. When you strive to gain something that another person already has in comparison to you, you thrive in a healthy environment. Instead of lamenting that you don't possess a skill, you can work hard to harness it.

3. Make the Shift from Competition to Cooperation.

Comparison can give us clues to understand what we like, what we want, and how to get it. And when we see what others have, we can convince ourselves that it is possible for us to aim and achieve the same thing too. Train your mind to understand that someone being better in comparison to you means you have a role model to look up to. If you see someone achieving something, then it is concrete proof that it can be done. By making the mental shift from competition to cooperation, we can change our views about a person from one of envy to one of appreciation. And we can harness the power of comparison to propel us to achieve our dreams.

4. Helps Us to Assess Ourselves

According to social comparison theory, we compare ourselves to others for expanding and honing our frame of reference for self-assessment. It gives a reality check when our objectives or the measures we take are not deemed as relevant. In some cases, as in 'upward' comparison, we also compare ourselves to others to boost our motivation by looking up to a more successful entity. In other circumstances, we indulge in 'downward' comparison to boost our self-esteem by focusing our thoughts on people who are in worse situations than us but are still thriving or at least making an effort to do so.

5. We gather Information about the People around Us

On a positive note, comparison can offer an information gathering framework. We may not even realise what we are capable of doing unless examples of other people appear before us. The example of other people attaining unimaginable heights of success can expand our sense of what we can envisage in future for ourselves. Seeing their struggles and success can help us anticipate the stumbling blocks that we will encounter and search for appropriate solutions for our endeavours. The more we crave to be like someone or even surpass their capabilities and achievements, the more we train and push ourselves to broaden our horizon of success and eventually reach the finishing line.

CHAPTER FOUR

MUST READ BOOKS FOR EVERY PROFESSIONAL

Sometimes there are books which inspire people to do something in their life. Then there are books which are written by corporate gurus which helps in people climbing the corporate ladder. Then are some books which inspire people to quit their jobs and encourage people to establish a start-up. There are some books which inspire people to do a whole lot of things which professionals want to do. Here, we would look into those books which are a must-read for professionals who are looking for inspiration to lead on the corporate leader or even be encouraged on their start-up.

- **Thinking, Fast and Slow by Daniel Kahneman:** Daniel Kahneman is a psychologist and a Nobel Prize Winner. In his book *Thinking, Fast and Slow,* the author breaks down an average person's thinking process into two sections. The first section is the impulsive and emotional side of a human being, and the second section is the one which is the logical and deliberate side of the human being. This book covers those situations and also provides nuggets of advice where it explains when a person should use the impulsive and emotional side, and when the person should use the deliberate and logical side of themselves. This also explains the need to use which section at the most appropriate time to take the most effective and better business decisions.

- **Discover Your True North by Bill George:** Bill George is a professor at Harvard Business School, and he has written this book *Discover Your True North* where he says that a person's style of working should be custom made according to his needs and capabilities whereas he shouldn't be forced to follow the style of leadership which doesn't suit them.

- **Giants of Enterprise Seven Business Innovators and the Empires They Built by Richard Ted low:** In his book, Richard writes about the CEO's of the past years who have risked it all and have managed to raise multi-millionaire empires. The Author includes all the plans, ideas and strategies behind the incorporation of these companies. The author takes the example of some well-known entrepreneurs who established well-known companies. Some of the companies that the author has made an example from are IBM founded by Thomas Watson, Henry Ford and Automobile Empire, Sam Walton and his supermarket chain Walmart, Inventor and founder of Intel Robert N. Noyce and the likes of other great minds who are sure to strike some inspiration to people who are looking for it.

- **Think and Grow Rich by Napoleon Hill:** Originally written in the year 1937, *Think and Grow Rich* was written as a self-help book or in other words, a book on self-improvement. The author has studied the behaviour and habits of the people who have amassed fortunes and created thirteen of his laws which the author believes that every person should follow to propel a person onto greater heights and control the thoughts of negativity and instead encourages the reader to focus on the long term goals.

- **The Hard Thing About Hard Things by Ben Horowitz:** This book describes the struggles of running a business. Ben is one of the most respected entrepreneurs in Silicon Valley and is the Co-Founder of Andreessen Horowitz. In his books, he talks about his struggle to keep his company working. The book covers the things which would go wrong and then about how to clean up the mess that the company has created. The author also speaks about his mentors. The book also focuses on the harsh situation and pressurised situation a CEO has to go through. This is a must-read book for any manager or even anyone interested in the workings of a start-up company.

- **The 4-Hour Workweek: Escape 9-5, Live Anywhere and Join the New Rich by Timothy Ferris:** The author talks about a lifestyle where a person can live a life which includes relaxation and luxury. The author challenges the old concept of settling down and retirement and is critical about the rat race that a person is trapped in their whole life. The book guides the reader with the steps to finding the perfect work-life balance. The author explains how he has managed to break away his hectic 80-hour per week routine and now works for merely 4-hours and earns as much in a month, as much as he used to make per annum.

- **Zero to One by Peter Thiel with Blake Masters:** This book is written by Peter Thiel, who is a well-known and respected entrepreneur and investor, guides the reader into figuring out new ideas required for creating original things and building start-ups. The book also explains the need to find new ideas and not mingle around inventing the same thing which has been developed. The book pushes the reader to think about new approaches to build up their start up.

CHAPTER FIVE

What is Change Management?

Change management is an approach to deal with the transition of an organisation's principles or any transformation in one's personal life. The purpose of change management is to employ strategies to help people to adapt to the change. For the change management process to be effective, it must consider how the changes or adjustments will impact processes,systems and employees in the organisation.Arrangements must be made for planning and testing, communicating a change, for scheduling and implementing change as well as for documenting a change.

How to Manage Changes in Personal Life

1. Visualise a Great Future

No matter what change you are going through, dream a compelling future for yourself. Create a vision board with images that represent aspects that fulfil your life. To translate those to reality, you need willingness, belief and commitment.

2. Understand your Emotions

People who go through change, encounter myriad emotions. The Five Stages of Grief that we go through while under stress are:

a. **Denial**- Denial is a human defense mechanism, where you are unable to accept the facts and the situation.
b. **Anger** –You might be angry with anyone, including yourself. Anger triggers feelings of anxiety, irritation and embarrassment.
c. **Bargaining** – In this stage, you start looking for alternatives. It is common to want to share your story with others to find meaning and even to search for people with similar situations to appease yourself.
d. **Depression** – Depression can make you distance yourself from others. You feel overwhelmed, a lack of energy along with sadness, regret, fear and uncertainty.
e. **Acceptance** – In this stage, you accept the change and start to explore new options and alternatives.

3. Find Balance in Life

To be better acquainted with the change, strike a balance in your life. If you devote yourself fully to work, any change in the workplace becomes unbearable. However, if you have a good balance between your work and personal life, changes become easier to tackle.

4. Be True to Yourself

There are differences between things you want and those that you deserve. Be true to yourself and don't get blinded by what everyone else is chasing after. Expand your energy doing something only when both your heart and mind are in synchronization.

5. Have a Positive Mindset

The most important step to successfully manage a change is to have a positive mindset. You can't prevent a change from happening, but you can change your attitude towards the change. People who resist change have a very pessimistic outlook of the future and feel powerless. To positively react to a change, lead a happy, dynamic life free from cynicism.

How to Manage Changes in Professional life

1. Maintain a positive attitude

You have to be optimistic with a good attitude irrespective of the company and the people you are working with. Think about how you can best use your skills, experiences and networks to establish yourself. If you have a negative attitude, nobody will be comfortable working with you.

2. Recognise that change is constant

People go through several careers changes and jobs in their lifetime. One of the reasons why companies change their employees from one project or work environment to another is because it prevents you from getting bored in your current role and challenges you to work on projects that you haven't before.

3. Stay connected to previous co-workers

Never forget to keep in touch with people you have previously worked with. If they are staying with your previous group, you can always communicate with them to help you with a project. They can become pivotal in keeping you connected to your earlier group, whether you are in the same company or different company.

4. Communicate with others to learn about your New Role

After you have moved into or settled your new role, you should quickly find all of the important people that you can rely on and connect with them. Find those people who have already been in your role or worked in the same capacity and get them to teach you everything you need to know so you can get up to speed and quickly enhance your performance. Become good at asking questions because the more you know, the better equipped you will be in handling your tasks and the easier your life will be. If you wait too long to reach out to them, your performance will start to lack, and people will begin to notice.

5. Be Optimistic although you are not Happy

No matter whether you like your new role or not, you need to make the best of your situation. You never know what opportunities the new change in your life might bring for you. You might also move again soon after starting in your new role. Think about the tasks that you prefer doing in your new role and how to best use your strengths to your advantage and increase your performance.

CHAPTER SIX

RELATIONSHIP BETWEEN ENGLISH SPEAKING AND CONFIDENCE.

Speaking a language in utmost confidence requires the proper hold to the language. Stuttering, taking breaks, stammering could come in the way of a person's confidence while speaking the language. For confidence in a language, the person would need to find the silver lining between learning the language itself and to present the topic to the audience. In speaking a language, confidence is important to communication and is a deciding factor of how others perceive us and how they judge us. This is also a factor through which we judge people based on their grasp on the language.

This is because it not only does define how a person expresses themselves but also shows how we work, how the person interacts with a person and the hunger to pursue a person's goals in their life. In the language English itself, confidence comes from successfully stringing together a group of words with correct grammar. Some of the beginners in the language think that they would have the confidence in speaking the language fluently themselves. But the main problem of human beings is that they forget the only thing that makes them fluent speaker. Making mistakes and learning from them.

There is a small misunderstanding that people have. That fluent speaker can naturally have a grasp in understanding any language. But it isn't the truth. Because even the people who are fluent in the English language weren't always this fluent, they did have their share of imperfection and mistakes, which made them learn the ropes of the language. The primary which is required for confidence in a language is to remain self-awareness. Once a person is aware of themselves, then they can observe and fix their mistakes quite often. This could play a huge role in improving a person's confidence and their grasp on the language. This could a huge step into helping a person gain confidence. And in general, there are few certain steps which can be used to improve a person's speaking skills which could further impact their confidence in a positive way.

- **Mentally visualise the words:** Before speaking, create a mental draft about how the person is going to start the conversation with. This could not only help the person in knowing the right things to say at the right time but could also help in boosting the confidence of a person. This practice could also help in looking into mistakes and rectifying it and clearing out any unwanted elements in the sentences the person intends to speak.

- **Practise speaking speeches:** A person could also boost their confidence by practising their speeches in front of the mirror. This could also help them prepare their speech and sentences, but also help them in checking out their body language and posture. This could also help in better presentation and better line delivery. This can also help them in perfecting the lines which they think are tough for them to speak up.

- **Think positively:** A person would feel confident in their language only when they think positively about themselves. Having cold foot is normal, but adding fuel to the fire never worked in favour of any person. That is the reason why having a positive attitude and a positive attitude to think about a person's upcoming project would help them in gaining confidence and speak the language in much more fluency and easiness. Thinking about things like themselves failing in speaking, fluently will put an abrupt pause to a person's confidence.

- **Update your Vocabulary:** Instead of using the same words in everything, the person could use different words to mix thing up. This would also add up to the person's dictionary but could also be further used in future for any other purpose. This can also lead to an increase in a person's confidence because they could remember these new words and then use maybe improve them.

- **Listen to podcasts, Read Books:** The best way to learn new words and keep using them to create meaningful sentences. This could also help in framing more sentences about certain topics. Learning new things have always helped a person in boosting a person's confidence. And looking through books also helps in a person look into learning the punctuation, grammar and proper sentencing. And meanwhile, podcasts can also help in teaching a person on how to transition from one sentence to another. This can help the person in learning about how to progress with a conversation.

Confidence is a skill which may be tough for some of the people to master. This is because a person is under confident in themselves. The only thing which could help them is to believe in themselves. Because having confidence in the person would only help the person in gaining confidence in other endeavours.

CHAPTER SEVEN

HOW TO CONDUCT AN ONGOING DEBATE AT THE WORKPLACE?

The debate is one of the best discussion methods used in schools, colleges and corporate workplaces. The debate is an oral discussion between two groups. One group speaks in favour of the main issue, while other groups provide different facts by being against the topic. Debate, as per the Dictionary of Oxford, is a professional discussion on a specific matter in a public gathering or assembly, in which the counter-party put up arguments and which usually concludes with the vote. The debate can be between a person or groups. Each team is provided sufficient time to structure and prepare their presentation. The team in support of resolution is called the positive side or proposition. The team against the decision is called negative side or opposition.

Importance of Debate at workplace

The debate can be an intimidating event when conducted at a workplace. It can make the environment heated, and things can get a bit serious. But debates are critical in the workplace to allow people to voice their worries. During a debate in the workplace, employees can raise their concerns on the topic. At the same time, other employees will throw light on the positive sides of the topic. Observing a debate carefully will guide a manager about the things that need to be a change in the organisation. Employees often show their dissatisfaction subconsciously during the debates.

Another good point is that employees are mostly trying to convince each other about the good and bad sides of the issue. They can analyse and have a better understanding of the issue without intervention from management.

Conducting a healthy office debate

The debate is a risky event if not organised properly. It can lead to disputes and peace disruption. So, you need to ensure certain factors for conducting productive and fruitful debates in the workplace.

- **Decide the right people for participation**

A lot of people in the debate will reduce the efficiency of the debate as the confusion will increase, and no conclusions will be made. It will also be hard to control them. Having less will make the debate inefficient. You should choose the right number of people depending on the topic. Having previous debate experience will tell you that 4-5 members in a team are sufficient to know different mind sets and make a proper conclusion. After deciding the number, you need to choose the target people that should participate. You can conduct a debate for people who do not communicate much in regular office days or conduct a debate for a particular department. The type of people should vary depending on the topic you have.

- **Deciding the topic**

The topic you choose should be something participants can relate to. Since we are talking about workplace debate, you should keep the topic formal. You can hold a debate on the credibility of a client, performance of machines, future predictions of the market, and so on. Debates are meant to benefit both employees and firms. Decide a topic that allows participants to speak what is on their mind, to give real feedback and to bring out the weaknesses in the system. The topic should be decided in a way that both sides have enough to talk about. For instance, you cannot keep the topic "Should the company put up proper environment-friendly machines?" This is a total, yes. The only point Opposition side will have a higher cost. The manager should keep a topic that is debatable for an extended period.

- **Have a moderator**

A moderator is the supervisor of the debate event. Moderators are essential for maintaining the integrity of debate and preventing conflicts. The moderator will intervene when the discussion starts going off the topic. Moderator also helps in keeping the heat low. This means calming down both sides when they start taking topics personally. A moderator will also ask questions and keep the participants engaged. Choosing the right moderator is crucial too.

- **Give guidelines and advice before the debate**

Participants should be brought together and given proper guidelines about the right debating style. Make it clear to them that every argument should be based on facts. Opinions should be allowed as long as they do not hurt other's sentiments. Advise the candidates not to take the topics personally. Employees should know that the debate is for the mutual benefit of the organisation. Therefore, there is no right and wrong side. Being right or proving someone wrong should not be the aim of the debate.

- **After debate measures**

Employees should be appreciated for participating in the debate. If there were any conflicts and disputes during the debate, it is the responsibility of management to resolve that conflict immediately after the debate is over.

The debate is an excellent way of involving employees in the decision-making process. It can also be used to improve the bonding between them. However, this is only possible when the debate is healthy and nurturing.

CHAPTER EIGHT

HOW TO PREPARE ACTIVE DECISION MAKERS IN THE WORKPLACE.

In any organisation, there come various situations where a person is required to make some crucial decision before implementing an extensive plan. This could mean that the person should step up as a leader and not crack under the heavy pressure of making the decision which benefits the employees and the pleases the employer. There are many different types of decision makers. Some of the decision makers usually use logic and use sound rationale to make decisions while others go with their gut instinct to make decisions. They even have highly creative ways to find a solution to the problem and go ahead with their choice, but they are left speechless on why they took the decision, whether they work or not.

Some of the decision makers are confident individuals who are knowledgeable and are experienced in making the right decision under pressurised situations while some crack under pressure and are generally confused about the outcome. When they are given the location to which they have to bring up the decision to make a decision, they struggle in building one on the fear that 'if' they are going to be wrong and start over thinking about the outcome even before the result is favourable or not.

There are some key points through which an employee could take the right decision if they are tasked with it:

- ***Provide enough information:*** Training and educating the person about the matter would be a good step towards making the employee understand what the most sought-after decision is. It helps the employee think more about the decision and add his ideas to it. This not only boosts the confidence of the employee but also makes sure that they do not make any rash and illogical decision, which they may regret later.

- ***Encourage the employee to take a decision:*** There are people who even after the most training, fail to come with a conclusion and come up with cold feet. This happens mostly because the employee isn't confident in themselves and second guess their decision. Instead of forcing the employee and causing more nervousness for them, it is recommended to give them time and then let them say whatever decision they have in their mind and then listen to it. Even if it isn't perfect, add a bit more ideas to support the employee's decision and make sure not to breathe down their neck.

- ***Success is primary; perfection isn't:*** Most employees are probably bad in decision making because they think that they wouldn't be able to achieve the perfect decision. They also over think the consequence of what would happen if they aren't perfect. But they do not think about the success of their decision.

- ***Weigh all the alternatives:*** When the decision is being made, think about all the parameters which will affect the decision. Some key factors of decision making should be the impact of the decision on the organisation which the employee works for, its effect on fellow employees, the ethics of the office, whether this decision is beneficial and supportive to other decisions and whether it could be a deal breaker in terms of the future decision.

- ***Procrastinating won't help:*** Waiting for the right time, providing an excuse to delaying the decision making, postponing the decision will not help the employee because eventually, the employee would have to come up with a decision in the end and there is a high chance that they would panic and make the wrong call. Therefore, the employee should make sure that they don't take too much time into making a decision. Even though they can take some time to think about the decision, the decision should be swift.

- ***Implement the decision:*** After everything is done and said, the employee should go ahead with the decision and have no regrets with their decision.

- ***Contribute to the implementation:*** The employee would have made a decision and given it a go ahead. But if the decision should come into full effect, the employee should also help in regulating the work and also contribute to the execution of the idea to make sure that they are in sync with the decision the employee had in their mind.

- ***Analyse the impact of the decision:*** Now, overthinking isn't something which will help in any situation. But analyse the decision the employee has taken. They should be ready to think about how their decision could impact future decision making in their organisation. Most of the decision taken usually benefit the organisation. Make sure to check every loophole and utilise every opportunity and identify the threats and work around them to come to a fruitful decision.

Ultimately, the employee needs to realise that not everyone can be pleased with their choice. Some may feel that the employee took the wrong call. But ultimately, the employee should make sure that the decision they take shouldn't be partial to themselves or any particular individual. The welfare of fellow employees and the organisation should be taken into consideration, and the employee shouldn't make any decision for personal gain.

CHAPTER NINE

HOW AN ATHLETE CAN INSPIRE A PROFESSIONAL TO BECOME SUCCESSFUL

While many of us can't run a 100-metre dash in 9.58 seconds or dunk on a 10-metre ring, witnessing events like them, do inspire most of us. As professionals working the whole year, most of us don't expect to have the physical prowess or fitness athletes maintain. But the key is to relate to the passion they possess and motivate yourself for the betterment and to achieve your dreams.

International athletes and sports, in general, are known to entertain and fascinate most of us for their luxurious lifestyles and thus have made a myth popular- that it is a glamorous life full of pillows and that they get paid for playing games. This couldn't be farther from the harsh reality that athletes endure the same brutal world as we do, and fame isn't what it seems to be. From these struggles, professionals can always learn from athletes by getting into the right mind set with the following lessons:

- ***Hard work done now can never be a waste down the line***

Climbing a mountain might be one of the most difficult tasks you can learn, but once you master climbing a mountain, it'll still feel easy. The practice and hard work are done for any work are sure to make you better and help out in one way or another. Any true athlete will always tell you that you can't work around hard work. There are no shortcuts sure to work for you. All you can do is make efforts here and now to reap its benefits in the future.

- ***The odds against you don't matter, and nothing is impossible***

Whether it is a modest upbringing, a career-threatening injury, or an ideal situation where can't seem to get it started, athletes are bent on trying to prove the skeptics wrong. They learn to get charged up by non-believers (or haters as the millennials call it), they possess the power to beat adversity as no one else does. Wherever others see the concern, they see an opportunity to do something no one else can.

- ***Limitations can only stop you if you let them***

If you reject your limitations, you may realize that your body will provide you with way more than you ever thought possible. Athletes also use mental image techniques before they contend with blowing away limiting thoughts with the power of imagination. Rather than that thinking about failures, they see themselves succeeding. . No matter what, don't place yourself into a class. You will lose your focus and start believing that you may never be as quick or as bold as others, however giving anything time can work wonders. Learn to reject the limitations life has instructed you to accept and dream big.

- ***Big dreams need focused plans to succeed***

Dreaming big isn't all that's needed. Even the laziest of the employee can dream about working in a big name company while lying on the couch. You also need to plan how you want to get there meticulously. Athletes don't just work out randomly with hopes of a bulkier or leaner body. They plan their workouts strategically to get the most out of them. This planned mixture of preparation and hard work is the key to success.

- ***Recognize the excuses you make to yourself and eliminate them***

There are excuses we make to others to delude them, but the worst excuse is one made to yourself. We lie to ourselves to sit in our area of comfort and avoid taking opportunities because it would be easier. These excuses are just a way to cover up our hidden fear of failure or other deep-rooted fears. This can be stopped by recognising when you're deluding yourself and acting on it. You might think you're too old or too skinny or too stupid to do something, but you need to take inspirations from athletes that prospered under worse conditions. Everyone has a reason not to start; you need to find one to make yourself take that tough step and go for it.

- ***Have a single-minded approach towards your goal***

Athletes have a single-minded devotion to work for what they want to achieve. They don't look for half-assed substitutes or just a better alternative, rather work to get to the place that they have passion for. They are thus dedicated to creating their dream of winning reality, and they banish any risk of a backup from their mind. This focus on the hunger to only settle for that ultimate success is what distinguishes a true athlete or successful professional from a failed one. This is a pattern found in everybody from Nikola Tesla to Einstein or even Bill Gates. If you wish for the ability to follow your dreams, you need to push aside all the alternatives.

CHAPTER TEN

HOW MENTAL HEALTH MAKES A DIFFERENCE IN YOUR PERSONAL AND PROFESSIONAL LIFE

There is a huge and evident impact of mental illness all over the globe. With our busy and high-pressure lifestyles, the mind has started to break down faster than our body. Mental health problems are becoming one of the most common and widespread contributors to disease and disability. Even now, 5 of the 10 leading causes of disability worldwide are mental health problems. They are as important and blatant in rich countries as in the poor ones and are seen growing in people irrelevant of their age, gender or social status. Furthermore, scientist and analyst predict that these problems are sure to increase dramatically in the future.

The burden of these mental health disorders on health and productivity have always been neglected and underestimated. Those that suffer are considered weak and not treated the same as people undergoing a physical disorder. This trend is slowly improving with the outreach of social media and productive journalism on the issues. With these problems gaining popularity in the mainstream mental health is no longer considered a joke among the common consumer.

The impact of mental health problems in the workplace has serious effects not only on the victim but also the company. No company can perform to its full potential with its employees suffering mental health issues. Things like performance, rates of illness, workplace accidents and turnover are all affected by an individual's mental health status.

Job stress and the effects of deteriorating mental health at the workplace

One of the most visible effects of your mental health can be seen in the workplace. Job Stress is a major contributor to the deteriorating conditions of most people's mental health. Job stress may be defined as the harmful physical and emotional response that happens once the needs of the work you're doing don't match your capabilities, resources or desires.

Some potential causes of work-related stress are overworking, lack of clear directions, surreal deadlines, lack of decision-making, job insecurity, isolated operating conditions and inadequate child-care. Though harassment and discrimination are usually excluded from lists of job stressors, they need to be included in any comprehensive analysis of the causes of work stress. Harassment could be a massive agent for girls within the workplace, and discrimination could be one for ethnic minorities. A number of the effects of stress can also cause physical ailments along with mental state problems like depression can be related to an increased rate of suicides.

In developing countries, there is increasing concern regarding the health impact of job stress due to the long and sometimes dangerous work hours employees are made to work for their pay cut. For example, an increased risk of work-related accidents and diseases has been observed in South-east Asian countries that have expanded their industries massively in recent times. In most countries, no specific laws are addressing the impact of job stress on an employee. But most countries do have at least minimum standards for safety and health at the workplace that need to be followed. These standards tend to focus on the physical effects of the workplace and do not factor in the psychological and mental health aspects of working conditions.

Adverse Effects of mental health problems in your personal life

Your professional life isn't the only one affected by your mental health as you can see the effects in your personal life as well. With mental health being this forgotten depression has become a widespread disease of the likes of smallpox in the olden times. It is predicted that by 2020, it will be the second largest disease burden worldwide. It goes beyond saying that depression isn't just "being sad" and can have adverse effects on your daily life as it turns completely colourless and you see no way out. These burdens can only be fixed with better awareness and people understanding how it affects them.

- It has been proved without any level of doubt that mental health is just as important as physical health if not more so as the former can even because the latter to deteriorate. Forex, depression is known to lead to heart and vascular diseases.
- Mental disorders affect a person's day to day behaviour like not eating sensibly, not exercising or getting enough sleep, increased tobacco and alcohol use, not being able to engage in sexual activates and all these habits can lead to an increased risk of physical illness.
- It can also lead to social problems like unemployment or breaking families apart and drug abuse or giving a person an affinity towards crime.
- Your immune system doesn't function properly if you don't let it. As seen in the power of placebos, the brain is an important factor in your recovery, and with poor mental health, your immune system suffers from performing.

CHAPTER ELEVEN

HOW TO BE A MOTIVATOR FOR SUCCESS

Success is a hard-earned fruit. Every individual aspires to attain success in their life, but few are truly able to reach the zenith point of success. To be successful in life, a person needs to strive the hardest even in darkest times, keep going even when there seems to be no hope. Successful people have toiled hard like never before to fulfil their dream. The secret to this persistence is motivation. And no one can be a better motivator than you. There is a recurring pattern to successfully motivating oneself. Even when you have, the following tips will help you to stay afloat.

Ways to Motivate for Success

1. Get serious

Get serious and do not fool around anymore. Decide to reach the top. Until now, you might have thought about it but never taken a step. Make your mind to go all the way to the top, and your life will take off. The moment you decide that you are going to be best at what you do, you embark on the most extraordinary journey towards success.

2. Know your limiting step

Figure out the aspects that are limiting you from achieving your target. Find out the qualities that people who have succeeded in your field possess and check mark those that you do not. Essentially, all you need to do is find what's keeping you stuck and what you need to do to get going again. Once you have determined the critical limiting step, your path becomes clear.

3. Get around the right people

Sort out the people who are important to you. Associate yourself with people who have been a winner in their fields. People who have plans and high aspirations will always exude positive vibes and inspiration to follow their footsteps. Filter out the toxic people from your life. Those who do nothing but lament and complain emit negative vibes. They can be detrimental to your success.

4. Stay focused on the big picture

Yes, admittedly, there will be days when work will be boring. You can feel irritated when tasks are repetitive, or you have a hundred things to do on your checklist. The easiest option is to feel frustrated and give up. Or you can stay focused on the big picture. Convince yourself that your task might be repetitive, but it is important. It will take you further along your career. Keep your eye on the big picture, and no job ever will feel boring or unimportant.

5. Talk nicely to yourself

Practice talking to yourself with motivational inner dialogues. Convince yourself through self-talk that you are living the best days of your life and that you love your job. Make yourself believe that all the hard work will never go to waste. Say to yourself where you want to be in future. Remember that your past might not be in your hands, but you are the sole person in charge of your future.

6. Get going

Develop a sense of urgency that will make you unique. The faster you move, the better you get in doing your job and hence, the more you like yourself. With increased self-acceptance come heightened self-esteem and a sense of discipline. Keep on persisting until you become unstoppable.

7. Get active

You cannot be motivated if you are not in a good mood. Pushing yourself physically is highly beneficial for intellectual development. Research has shown that exercising for thirty minutes can increase levels of serotonin, dopamine, and norepinephrine in your brain, which can help to reduce stress and prevents the onset of depression. Taking a walk early in the morning or working out will keep you relaxed throughout the day, less stressed out with a clearer ability to think. Also working out is a great way to test your boundaries and keep you healthy. It will make you re-evaluate the limits of your capabilities.

8. Brainstorm your ideas and visualise them

Your great ideas will come to your mind when you least expect them. Of course, not all the ideas that come to you will be good or fruitful. No matter what, good or bad, useful or not, write down the ideas revolving in your head. Eventually, after you have jotted down a billion views, you have a high chance if discovering that at least one of your designs is good. It is incredibly motivating to realise that you can be the source of great thoughts too. The next step is to visualise those ideas. Close your eyes and imagine transforming those ideas into reality. Think about all the achievements that you are going to make. Think about the impact that you will be able to make. Think of the future that you are going to build.

CHAPTER TWELVE

HOW TO BE QUICK "FIT" IN BUSY SCHEDULE

Hustle every day! Something everybody has heard at least once in their lives, especially if they are as active a member on YouTube as I am. In this day and age, everybody has their thing. Everybody is busy with something or the other. Everybody has engagements, plans and things they need to take care of, daily. Amongst all these, a person forgets the most important thing, to take care of the vessel through which the work is done, your body. To stay fit in your life is an utmost important thing to care of, among everything else. Because if you are unwell, all your work gets delayed automatically. How to take care of your body when you have a busy schedule? That exact question we'll be answering here today.

Things to follow:

Staying fit doesn't only mean staying away from diseases and illness. Staying fit also means being in the said BMI, not being overweight or underweight, and having a healthy and toned body without the presence of any harmful substances in the body.

Most of the people nowadays, even busy people, go to the gym for a quick workout session of an hour or so, which is why the majority of the people suggest gym as a suitable option for losing weight and staying fit. Other outdoor options for staying fit that include an entire body fitness regime are swimming, dancing and playing sports like football or basketball. These help you to stay fit and tones your body to decrease the muscle fat. Along with fitness, such outdoor routines help you to stay fit internally as well. They increase your heart rate and smoothen the circulation of blood and digestion problems are eliminated, to name a few.

What happens if somebody doesn't want to go to the gym, but wants to stay fit? That is as much possible as it is with a gym. Below mentioned are some suggested ways to stay fit in a busy schedule.

- Walking is the most basic movement, but it helps a lot in the day to life. It helps you reduce a lot of calories and also helps you build your leg muscles and calf muscles. And it is also something that can be done while going or coming back from your workplace since the time for this gets included in the schedule of the day. A lot of times when you are on the phone, you can walk and talk. This also helps as you won't feel the exhaustion due to the phone call, but you'll be burning calories without wasting extra time there.

- There is YouTube, as I mentioned earlier, and floating on YouTube are a lot of workout videos that let you stay at home and do them as per procedure, like sit-ups, crunches, lunges, and many other types of regimes. These workout plans don't need a gym or special equipment. These can be done for 15-30 minutes every day.

- As I said with walking, taking the stairs also accounts for it. Whenever you are reaching the workplace before time, taking the stairs instead of the elevator will do wonders. It burns your calories and along with it helps to keep you fit. It is much more effective than jogging.

- You can buy small equipment, like dumbbells, skipping ropes and other forms of small fitness equipment that can be easily stored and used at home. These can be used more for toning of your body and improving your biceps and other muscles of the body. If you don't want to spend on equipment, then you can get creative about things. You can see around your house and lift things that might seem effectively heavy to you for mini workout sessions as well.

- Exercising every day and jogging every morning is something that can be followed for, and the benefits of this are huge. Morning is the best time to do so as it lets you into the day feeling positive.

- If you want to stay fit by changing your eating habits, then eating boiled and less spicy or less oily food is a great start for it. Eating almonds every morning and juices as soon as you wake up helps on the regular intake of nutrients and also sharpens the brain keeping the body fit without the unnecessary accumulation of calories and other harmful substances.

Conclusion:

Your body is your temple, and you are the one who is solely responsible for its care and safety. Unfit bodies are the leading causes of illness in people. Hence, please take care and keep yourselves fit. As it is commonly said that health is the real wealth you should be seeking for; hopefully, after reading this, you will give a minute or two thinking about your habit and health in day to day life.

CHAPTER THIRTEEN

HOW TO DEVELOP A SELF-REGULATION STRATEGY FOR SURE SUCCESS

Self-Regulation is a personality trait important for people of all ages. Self-regulation is the state of regulating or controlling one's emotions, behaviours, physical actions, and mind set with no help from external parties like friends or family. It is the skill to stop disruptive impulses and emotions when conditions are unfavourable. In simple words, Self-regulation is control of oneself by oneself. Self-regulation can refer to the control activities of different organisms. In humans, the most important control is psychological Self-regulation. Psychological Self-regulation is not similar to suppressing feelings or emotions. It helps in adapting positively to achieve success in any condition.

According to Albert Bandura, Self-regulation is a continuous process with the following functions-

- Monitoring the behaviour in real time and understanding the influences and consequences of your behaviour on other people.
- I am judging their behaviour based on personal beliefs and personal standards.
- I am reacting to my behaviour by taking corrective action.

Importance of Self-regulation

Self-regulation is a skill that helps you to think before acting. It helps in incorporating patience, calmness, and a habit of taking sufficient time to act. Self-regulation makes you calm and composed. A person with low self-regulation is bound to make mistakes more often. Humans thrive because they can think well. When a frustrated person acts up, he loses the self-regulation standards and goes on a rampage of mistakes.

Self-regulation is a sign of maturity. Any adult who lacks these skills will feel a lack of confidence. One shall have lower self-esteem because of the hastiness in behaviour. This is not a problem with people having a high self-regulation system developed since childhood. Self-regulation also prevents you from doing anything that goes against your values and beliefs. And most importantly, Self-regulation helps to face failures and still have a positive outlook on the world. It helps to tackle failures with calm and maturity. This gift of Self-regulation will be helpful in every field of life.

The right time to work on Self-regulation development

The best time for developing Self-regulation skills in a person is the childhood period. A young child is like a blank notebook. The brain can be taught easily and properly. Soft skills like Self-regulation, self-discipline, confidence, and communication should be incorporated right from childhood. Teenage is also receptive to new learning. As humans reach adult age, the brain becomes stubborn and occupied with many beliefs and ideas.

Changing these thoughts and introducing Self-regulation skill is more difficult. A person is less receptive to psychological learning. A lack of self-regulation development in childhood can cause the inability to manage feelings. It can even cause severe problems like mental disorders or substance abuse.

How to Develop Self-Regulation?

Several strategies can be used to develop strong self-regulation skills. The task is easier in childhood. However, you can start at any age with proper determination.

- **Being mindful**

Being attentive and aware is the first step to Self-regulation. Mindfulness is a state of awareness where the person is living every moment with high consciousness. Being mindful is the way to live a disciplined and happy life. You will always regret the moments when you lost awareness and control. Mindfulness helps in keeping your mind and actions in sync. This reduces your behavioural and emotional mistakes. According to 27 studies done in this field, Mindfulness has a positive effect on attentiveness. This attentiveness helps in understanding their feelings and tackling adverse situations.

You should know that every situation gives you two options. The approach or avoid. They are also known as flight or fight. Being mindful helps you to choose the option that suits your beliefs and personality.

- **Cognitive Reappraisals**

The name suggests the meaning of this process. Cognitive reappraisal is the process of analysing thoughts and patterns with a positive outlook. It is a way of adaptive thinking. People often forget about the importance of having cognitive reappraisal systems in personality. An example of cognitive thinking is-

Suppose your friend is not answering your calls and not reading your texts. A self-regulated person will think that the friend must be busy. While a person with weak cognitive reappraisals skills will conclude that the friend does not want to talk or does not like him. The second thinking pattern does no good to the saturation. Instead of jumping to negative conclusions, you need to jump on positive ones. This helps in keeping your brain tension free and your relationships healthy.

There are other techniques for developing rock-solid self-regulation principles. A person can start incorporating acceptance habits and problem-solving outlook in daily life. Several negative habits damage your Self-regulated lifestyle. Avoidance, over thinking, depression, worrying, and suppressing emotions are some activities that you should completely avoid.

CHAPTER FOURTEEN

HOW TO LIVE LIFE AND ENJOY HOLIDAYS FULLY

The holiday season is knocking at your door and with it comes some great opportunities for refreshment. This is your time apart from workplace stress and unending project work. How should you spend that time? No matter what you do, you must ensure to spend the holiday break in such a way that will improve your health and your mood, enhance your brain function, and improve your productivity at work later. To enjoy holidays fully, you need not go on long vacations to exotic tourist destinations every time. It can be as simple as a day out with family or a barbecue with your friends. Experiencing new things such as starting a new exercise regimen, taking up meditation, or going to a spa are very beneficial to do. To get most of the benefit out of your holiday break, here is a list of what you need to do:

1. Unplug from work.

Unplugging from work does not mean not checking emails or responding to messages for an entire week. Not only will this cause a constant worry and turmoil inside you but might also create havoc at the workplace. Instead, find a possible workaround during the holidays. Schedule yourself for one hour every morning or every afternoon for work. Check and respond to emails, answer to all sorts of work-related queries, and exchange updates on urgent projects in this time. This will not only give you ample time for mental relaxation and enjoyment but also will send a strong message to your co-workers and employees. It is important to understand that it is okay, and in fact, much needed to take a break from work, and while you are on vacation, you must be considered unavailable except for serious issues.

2. Get plenty of sleep.

Sleep is extremely important to our work and our mental health, and sadly, most of us don't get enough of it during our working days. Studies show that vacations improve our overall wellbeing if we make sure to get enough sleep that we need during our time off from work. This also means making sure you have a comfortable and relaxing place to sleep where you get sufficient rest without being disturbed.

3. Try out a new skill.

There is a good amount of evidence that learning something new such as a new language or musical instrument, has enormous power to boost the brain. Thus, make sure that you spend some of your vacation weeks trying out a new hobby or skill. It can be anything from a drone flying to paddle boating to yoga to water colour painting. Even if you might never climb on a paddle board again or pick up a paintbrush ever again, you will have rejuvenated your mind in new ways that will forge new connections in your brain. By extracting yourself out of your usual mental patterns, you will make sure that when you go back to work, you are refreshed.

4. Do something memorable.

Two of the biggest benefits of a vacation are the excitement and anticipation that comes beforehand and relishing all the happy memories of it afterward. All of us look back on spectacular vacations that we have taken, and every time we do, it makes us happy. You can venture out to create all kinds of wonderful memories. Plan to do something that you have never done before that you will deeply enjoy, even if it's just for one day of your vacation. You'll reap the benefits of these out of the ordinary experiences for a long time to come.

5. Spend time with family, friends, or community.

Another benefit of a vacation is that it strengthens relationships with your partner, friends, or family because you spend time with them and give them your attention. That is beneficial for you because science tells us that the more connected we are with loved ones and with the external community, the healthier and happier we are. Although this is important every time of year, it is largely needed during holiday time. Instead of being solitary in holiday times, spend it with your family, friends, and community.

6. Enjoy yourself.

The most important way to ensure your happiness and well-being during your vacation and the time afterward is to make sure you spend doing things that you truly enjoy. All the advice will go to waste if you cannot enjoy your vacation. Yes, admittedly holiday season which comes with family obligations, loads of travel and unpleasant weather conditions can be challenging, but you can overcome these petty barriers and truly enjoy it. You should not necessarily ditch your family commitments and traditions to make way for your entertainment but make sure to set aside some time to do something that will make happy.

CHAPTER FIFTEEN

HOW TO SAY "NO" WITHOUT ANY CONFLICT

In a society that patronises and supports yes-men, being firm and saying no without shame, fear or any remorse is an extremely tough task to achieve. There can be an array of situations where you are stuck in a condition where saying no can be awkward or can be taken in a bad light. Your friends are gathering for a vacation, and you'll have to give up on the work to take leave to join them? Or something as simple as trying your rookie niece/ nephew's cooked food? Do you have to always say yes in tough situations like these by putting the needs and expectations of others over yourself?

No! Of course not. But sometimes saying no to someone is easier said than done and this article will help you improve this problem most of us have to go through in life.

The Fear of saying No

Just like most fears of our lives, the fear of saying no comes from our childhood experiences and memories. What did your experiences tell you about the meaning of "yes" and what it meant to mention "no" while growing up?

It's vital to look at the teachings, each implicit and specific, you learned concerning these words and their meanings growing up. Did you learn that you had to mention affirmative to stay the peace? To avoid conflict? To not hurt the feelings of someone you cared about?. The answers to these questions can decide how what believes you're going to have when you grow up. Sadly, most of tend to hold onto our childhood beliefs, and hence we associate no with being dislikeable, unkind, or selfish. We feel that saying no will lead to us feeling humiliated or ashamed, and we will find ourselves alone and abandoned.

The point is before saying no you need to figure out the hidden agenda you're hesitating to say I in the first place. Once you know what the reason is, you should find a way to associate your "no" with something positive for the receiver. Think of it this way, rather than stalling someone and disingenuously saying yes and not pulling through later, you can consider saying no as a selfless and positive act as saying no now would save the receiver time and effort. Saying that you will consider something and then not following up can easily be more disappointed than a simple No said respectful

Of course, none of this is based in reality, and like most fears, you can see how nonsensical it is if you think about it. In our modern world, saying no is an everyday activity, and everyone should and does look out for themselves. A friend wouldn't just get up and abandon you if you said no to plans they made. They might be disappointed that things didn't go as they wished, but no one thinks about these decisions as you do yourself. In the same way for professional situations, being honest goes a long way rather than accepting everything thrown your way.

New perspectives to look towards to help you say No more easily

To indeed be able, to be honest with others and yourself, you need to change your beliefs and mind set on what it means to say no. You can do so by looking at the following ways to say no in a helpful, respectful, and healthy manner.

- When you say no to someone, you're telling them that they can do the same to you and it's alright if they do. This can be harder to execute when you're on the receiving end of this rejection but is the most crucial aspect to change within us. By letting someone execute their right of saying no without fuss, you open up the opportunity for you to get the same right without any judgment or pressure from others.

- As discussed above, saying no and putting someone off clears them up to look for alternatives and saves everyone involved precious time. The time that would be wasted if you made them wait for a flimsy and sudden no later.

- Learning to say what you genuinely think is excellent for mental health and will mean that you can avoid toxic situations that others might get stuck in. This healthy habit will lead to you feeling more fulfilled and happier with people you want to be with and working on things you want to work on. This means more time to work on yourself and less time wasting time on things you didn't want to sign up for in the first place.

- Ultimately saying nowhere, you need to leave you with an opportunity to say yes for something you want to do and leaves all parties involved with better protection of their boundaries and comfort. There needs to be mutual respect when you say no to someone or even if someone says no to you. This mutual comfort will mean you can have longer and healthier relationships with people be it professional or personal.

CHAPTER SIXTEEN

IMPORTANCE OF PUTTING YOURSELF FIRST

Often we forget to put ourselves first. Maybe this is because our parents, teachers, and elders taught us that it is selfish and that we should always be considerate and loving toward others. They taught us to put the happiness of others before our happiness and that we should selflessly work for others without thinking of self-benefit or care. We can only give to others that which we have within us. If we exhaust ourselves in giving our time and energy to others, we cannot invest in others after a certain period.

Hence, to balance our priorities, we must know what to do. It's time we learn how to put ourselves first. There are perfectly good reasons why we should learn to do that and now is the time to turn the page, be our priority and remember that you can unlock the key to happiness and good, healthy relationships by taking care of yourself and loving yourself first.

1. Everybody creates their happiness.

Your happiness is in your own hands. Sometimes by spending all our time trying to make somebody else happy, we end up making ourselves miserable. You cannot be responsible for someone else's happiness, and similarly, they cannot be responsible for yours.

2. It teaches people how to treat you.

People learn from the examples around them. If you put yourself last, everyone around you will do so. You will be expected to work for everyone else without receiving any favor or gratitude. So treat yourself the way you want somebody else to treat you and people's behavior toward you will change for the better.

3. It makes you more confident.

Learning how to put ourselves first reflects on our self-confidence, which improves our lives. Self-confidence means we value ourselves as much as everyone else does. The confidence we build makes a huge leap in improving our relationship with others. People like being around those who are comfortable with who they are.

4. Others will benefit from it.

If you are tired and exhausted and still want to please everyone, it will lead to nowhere but depression. If you are unhappy and burned out, take care of yourself, and pamper yourself before thinking about others. Once you have enough energy and you feel good, you will be useful to people.

5. People will stop taking you for granted.

Being ready to help is one thing, but letting people make you do things unwillingly is something you should never allow. When you stop saying a 'no' they take you for granted and don't appreciate anything you do for them. Never let anyone take advantage of your kindness.

6. You'll realize that not everyone deserves a place in your life.

The sooner you realize that some people are not meant to be in your life, the faster you learn a lesson. Life is complicated, as even without toxic people around you. Instead of mourning their loss, wave them goodbye.

7. It doesn't mean putting others last.

There is a significant difference between being selfish and putting yourself first. Being selfish means, you are, whereas putting yourself first means being as kind to yourself as to others. It means taking care of yourself to be a productive and better person. Loving yourself a little more than you love others is not selfish.

8. You are your hero.

Remember that you cannot rely on others to save you. True, misery hurts less when you share it with somebody who cares about you, but they can never solve the problem. You have to be your hero and lift yourself when you are down and get out of a critical situation.

9. Your romantic relationships will be better.

When we are in love, we forget that we need our own space and time to function better as a couple. Concentrate more on the quality of time spent together rather than on just being together the entire day. If you take time to do the things you like, you will feel more relaxed and will also ensure new and exciting topics for conversation rather than it being centered on one person. When you start feeling satisfied with yourself, your relationship with your partner will be deeper and better.

10. Your relationship with yourself will be better.

When you learn to put yourself first, only then will you be able to figure out the true essence of yourself. You will discover yourself in various ways and will value yourself more. You will be there for people who are important to you but will be able to draw the line when necessary. You will learn to be the master of your likes and dislikes that you had not explored because you kept putting yourself last.

CHAPTER SEVENTEEN

MOST IMPORTANT OFFICE SKILLS FOR PROFESSIONALS IN 2022

With the wide range of competition in the world, you might think about how you can get an advantage over your peers. This can be done by the general understanding of what skills and qualifications your field of work or dream industry needs. There are, of course, technical and tech-oriented skills and other human relationship and arts-oriented skills. You'll be shocked at how important these human-based skills have become in our world even more so than the science and tech-oriented skills.

Strengthening a soft talent is one among the simplest investments you'll be able to build in your career, as they never exit your mind and builds character. Plus, the increase of AI is just creating soft skills progressively necessary, as they're exactly the kind of skills robots can't automatise. Of course, you will always need to learn the necessary work-related skills as all talk, and no brain won't get you anywhere either. But, there are a few skills that can be generalised as the one very corporation wants in an ideal employee. So, what soft skills are corporations searching for most in 2019? They are:

Visualizing Information

Yes, you can get information and process it yourself. That's straightforward. However, do you have the knowledge and imagination to scan that data and explain it to others? If you visualise the info, you'll be able to express it to others better, and that's what employers need you to be able to do. You'll be able to tell the business executives as well as the public what your findings mean, and that's priceless to a company. This grants you the ability to communicate to the higher level of the sector as well as the general passer-by that might not know anything about the topic.

Creativity

There was a time when creativity and business used to be two separate worlds, as separate as oil and water. But those days are gone now, and with the rising saturation in all fields of work, everybody desires the creative, artistic force on their team to be able to investigate issues in new, distinctive ways with contemporary views. Employers also tend to look for creative people to help them think of new and fresh ideas for merchandise and services.

Complex Problem Solving ability

Here is another skill that grows and matures well in humanities students. They can find different perspectives to a problem and creatively look at better solutions for them. It is also important how we execute this the right way, and the step from thinking of the solution to applying it requires additional skills like your leadership qualities and communication skills. This problem-solving ability can be somewhat sharpened by playing video games and various types of puzzles.

Emotional Intelligence

Emotional Intelligence, or EQ, refers to; however, we can emotionally relate to an individual. With the increase in AI and machine learning, this is another skill that has come to the forefront and is a must have as having a high EQ means you can better relate to your clients and connect with them on an emotional level which a machine can't do and is what sets you apart.

Cognitive Flexibility

This doesn't refer to your ability to do gymnastics rather how flexible you are in changing up your conversational cues depending on the people you interact with. There should be a clear difference in the matter you present yourself in front of the CEO or with an intern. Cognitive flexibility can be the skill that helps you change up your sales tactic for each separate client and be the person that can be relatable to everyone.

People Management

This is another skill every employer wants in all of their employees. With everyone adept in computer management the more important skill now is people management as no matter how well you handle the files on your computer, you will need to be a good team member or leader to use those files and reach the final product needed. This is the field that dictates how well you can motivate your peers and make working fun for them all while having increased productivity from them. If you can help a corporation have happy employees, they will never hesitate to hire you.

Negotiation skills

This is another ability exclusive to humans and one that a machine can never hope to imitate. Negotiation is the centre of all business deals and is, therefore, a very important ability employer rummage for. Negotiation needs wonderful communication and debating skills and meshed with the psychological information you need it can be used to the greatest degree to maximize profits.

As you can see, the world has shifted, and with this focus on interpersonal and communication skills, you need to be sure to have these basic skills in your arsenal to secure the goals you seek in life.

CHAPTER EIGHTEEN

MUST HAVE LEADERSHIP SKILLS FOR PROFESSIONALS

Professionals today are expected to have a wide array of skills, be it ones related to their profession or ones that have become general and are just expected of them. Leadership is such a skill or responsibility that is expected of any professional, and there are a variety of sub-skills a good leader needs. So the question arises, what makes a good leader? And what are these leadership skills? It is clear that a leader requires a broad set of skills, but even then there is an excellent diversity in ways and styles to lead.

This means that there is no single "right" way to lead that is correct for every circumstance, and for a leader to be great, he has to be flexible enough to understand that. Adaptability is a significant feature of a leader and is something employers look for when looking for employees in leadership positions. Additionally, you should be able to deal with people positively and motivate them by generating enthusiasm in them. While Leadership by itself isn't a skill one can be taught, skills that make a good leader has can always be learned and practiced.

Skills every leader must possess

There are a variety of broad talent areas that are notably necessary for leaders. These include things like strategic thinking, communication, people management, amendment management, and persuasion and influencing.

- ***Strategic Thinking skills***
- Perhaps the foremost vital talent a leader needs and what remarkably distinguishes leaders from managers is to be able to think strategically. This means, in easy terms, having an inspiration or vision of wherever you would like to be and dealing with all the issues and problems to attain that.
- The best strategic thinkers see the big picture and aren't distracted by unnecessary problems or minor details. All their choices are seemingly sure to be a step that takes them nearer to where they want to be in that final picture. Of course, the ability to make a compelling vision isn't enough; they also need to be able to communicate it effectively to their followers; that is why communication skills are critical to leaders.
- Creating a vision isn't merely a matter of getting inspiration. Smart strategic thinking should be supported by proof, which means that having the ability to collect and analyze data from a tasty variety of sources. Knowing and understanding your market and your customers, and then using that data to support your strategic choices.

- ***People Management Skills***

Without followers, there are no leaders. Leaders thus want skills in operating with others on a regular and collective basis, and a variety of tools in their armory to handle a broad range of things. In explicit, leaders are a unit expected to inspire and encourage their followers.

One of the primary skills that new leaders must master is a way to delegate. This is often a fierce talent for several folks; however, done well; the delegation will provide team members responsibility and a style of leadership themselves, and facilitate them to stay driven.

Leaders and managers each should work together and perceive a way to build and manage the team. They have to grasp a way to recruit effectively. They additionally have to understand the importance of performance management, be it daily or to manage poor performance.

- ***Persuasion and Influencing Skills***

Finally, one specific space of communication that's particularly vital for leaders is having the ability to steer and influence others. Good leaders use a variety of tools for this. For the most part, persuasion and influence come from a person's confidence and body language. Of course, excellent communicational skills will come in handy too.As with everything practice makes perfect, and this is one of those skills that you can increase or gain only with training and experience.

- ***Change management and Innovation***

Change management might seem like a made up skill in front of communication and people management, but a leader is often most needed and valued at the times of change. As a leader, you must work unfazed by change and use every situation to the best possible outcome. This different thinking can only be achieved by introducing innovation into your approach.

Leadership Style

One of the foremost vital aspects of leadership is that not each leader is the same. There are many alternative forms of leadership. Take it into consideration that there is a significant difference between the boss and the leader; people thrive for leaders.

Different leadership designs apply to various individuals and unusual circumstances, and also the best leaders learn to use a significant form of maps.

There are many alternative models and styles of leadership. However, one of the famous ones are the ones stated in Daniel Goleman's Six Leadership designs. They include style like coercive, Pace-setting, affiliative, coaching, etc.

CHAPTER NINETEEN

PROFESSIONAL WAYS OF DOING SUCCESSFUL MULTITASKING

Have you ever found yourself trying to remember what you were doing while thinking about another task? Or emptily trying to remember what you were talking about while you lost your train of thought to something else? This is what multitasking or *attempted* multitasking looks like. With multitasking, if done incorrectly, you will probably end up losing focus on all the tasks you wanted to do and end up starting everything over again.

What is Multitasking, and how can it be achieved?

Multitasking, whether it be personal or professional, is what we do when we try to do more than one thing at the same time. So you might be wondering how your brain can work on two things at the same time. The real answer is: **It can't**. Our brain is designed to focus on only one thing at a time and trying to handle more reduces your efficiency and performance. Research has also shown that along with slowing you down multitasking can also lower your IQ.

So in the fast-paced lives, we live in, where sometimes multitasking seems like the only possible solution to your problems, how do you do the impossible?

How to Multitask Successfully

While multitasking at work isn't necessary or ideal, it sometimes does become a need when you're running late on things and need to take hold of the situation quickly. The real trick to multitasking is not to attempt to do random things together but rather planning your approach and how you're going to execute doing your work. Mastering multitasking successfully means using the 24 hours that everyone gets to the maximum extent. So the following tips can help you in mastering the art of multitasking professionally.

- ***Plan your next moves extensively***

The first and most important step for effective multitasking is to make a plan or set goals that you want to achieve. Without this step and deciding that you can do it randomly can mean more work for you than you started with. It takes well thought out planning to determine what tasks you need to do, by what time and assigning the correct order to all of them. This initial planning means when you get from one job to another, you won't just have to stop and start thinking from scratch how you want to do it. A great place to start having this habit is a to-do-list that you can assign yourself periods and goals in.

- ***Work on similar chores at the same time***

The easiest trick you can use to multitask effectively is combining tasks that have similarities among them and doing them at once. To jump from task to task successfully having them close together in theme and application makes it easier for you to retain your focus and can help you achieve them without thinking of new information and just relying on your short term memory for heightened effectiveness.

In a professional setting, this means doing simple things like clubbing similar clients together or providing similar clients similar marketing plans. This way, you will not waste any time, and both clients will be happy with the quick and effective work.

- ***Keep checking on your progress in tasks and goals***

This goes back to the point about planning your tasks but just planning it once and then going on about with work won't help you as you are bound to lose focus at some point. This is why you need to make sure now and then that you're on the correct path and keep working on completing that to-do-list or working for that goal. If at any point you think multitasking is getting in the way of a particular goal and you're not able to focus on it you can take small steps in that task alone while putting others on hold.

- ***Manage your distractions at work***

In our modern lifestyles, getting distracted is as easy as eating cake and can hinder the progress of the easiest tasks. Then, of course, getting distracted while juggling multiple tasks is a nightmare that no one wants to handle. This could mean something as simple as keeping your office door closed while working or working alone in the conference room to increase concentration. Your phone can be your greatest distraction and hence enemy in the workplace, so make sure you keep it off and only use it for personal reasons during the lunchtime. This will be especially important when working long hours, as your focus is sure to dwindle and the slightest of nudges towards a distraction will start looking very attractive.

- ***After completion, thoroughly review your work***

With everything done and your projects completed, it is still imperative that you take the time and review it thoroughly. This might seem like a waste of time, and everything multitasking was against in the first place, but the fact is not everyone can handle doing multiple tasks at the same time and completing them to perfection. This means you will make mistakes, and reviewing your work can help weed them out.

CHAPTER TWENTY

HOW TO GET A PROMOTION FAST IN YOUR ORGANISATION

In the corporate world, the only aim of an employee is to climb the corporate ladder and become successful in terms of position and money. It isn't tough to suggest yourself for a promotion, provided that the person has worked hard for the promotion, and the employer sees the work done by the employee. The employee should make sure that the boss should understand that the worker is doing all that they could do to earn the promotion. There are certainly some ways through which the employee could make themselves discovered.

- **Don't leave any work for the Boss:** It may or may not feel ironic in some way, but as mentioned, the best way to get noticed by the boss is to make sure that there isn't any work left for the boss to work for. This shows the boss that you could be trusted with the work that he has been entrusted with. And in turn, the boss would be able to work in more topics and could also recommend your name for any vital work to the higher-ups in the company, making you noticed for the work you did.

- **Lead a project from the beginning to the end:** Every organisation and company is on the lookout for human assets which are loyal to the work they are given. Consistency is a critical factor in any organisation. Owning up to any project from the start of the project to the end can show the company that you are consistent on the project and that you are loyal to the company. This could again work in your favour and not only would it get you noticed, but this could also mean that the company sees you as an indispensable asset and your reputation among the company would be increased.

- **Maintaining a positive demeanour:** There would be times where the company would be stressing the employees to work harder for them. The employees who intend to be promoted should keep a calm and relaxed demeanour and should have a positive attitude even if the things are not working in their favour. The employee should not crack under stress and do the task given to them and submit them under the deadline to find time to correct any small errors which may arise in the project. This could help in maintaining good relations with their superiors.

- **Make the Boss aware that you need a promotion:** Now that you have done what it takes to reach in the good books of the boss and the company, the employee has to approach the manager to speak about the promotion. Be humble, don't just demand it. The best strategy is to work your way of talking to your boss about the development. Because in some instances, the boss wouldn't have decided about your event. So it is advised that the employee provides subtle hints that they are ready for the promotion. Some organisation would stress on the fact that the next position is tough and challenging and would inquire if you are prepared for it. Be hungry and passionate to achieve the promotion.

- **Handle the work personally:** To give all of your talents into your work, it is advised that the employer should take the action as a personal task and should complete it like an own goal and put all their effort into it. Not only does it make sure that the work is complete and submitted on deadline, but it also makes sure that the work is near perfect and not botched.

- **Stay away from gossips and office politics:** Even though there is a formal term for it "Grapevine Communication," the employee should make sure that the employee should not be involved in these types of rumours. Even though it is necessary to listen to what is happening at the office, the best advice is to stay away, and this is because if the employee is caught spreading the unwanted rumours, then it could result in a bad reputation for the employee in the eyes of the management. And this could also contribute to the sense of untrustworthiness in the eyes of the administration.

- **Show Commitment:** The employee should show commitment to completing the project or the task was given to him by the management and should ensure that the employee completes it with utmost sincerity and loyalty. There shouldn't be any blanks left in the project.

- **Justify your promotion:** The employer and the management need to make sure if the employee is capable of the development. The employee should make sure that they do all the work that needs to be done to prove and show the management that they are eligible, and they are ready the earn their promotion.

CHAPTER TWENTY-ONE

RELATIONSHIP BETWEEN RISK AND SUCCESS

Many of life's greatest achievements propel us to go beyond our comfort zone and achieve the unthinkable. Be it onstage performances for artistes or investing money for the growth of your business, life's most rewarding experiences are a benefit of taking risks.

Many are turned off by the idea of taking risks. It is easier and more comfortable to sit back and wait for an opportunity. While the dreamers are sleeping and waiting for the best moment, the taker has grabbed the opportunity. Risk takers are likely to be more successful as they do not hesitate to take chances.

Reasons Why People Taking Risks Are Successful

1. **They experience Passion**

Mostly, adventurous people are the ones who take the risk. They have a burning zeal to reach new heights, and it empowers them to be creative with a winning spirit.

2. They Stand Out

People who take risks are bold and courageous. With courage also come confidence and the will to be persistent. This makes risk takers leaders as they are self-motivated.

3. **They gain Knowledge**

Knowledge is the key to success. Risk takers can garner understanding because they are willing to undergo a rigorous process to attain it. Through such experience, they can navigate in future and sail through troubled waters.

4. **They pursue Success**

Risk takers know that they have to chase and hunt for success. That is what they do while taking risks. Because risk takers actively seek success, they find many seemingly rare opportunities.

5. **They are not Afraid of Failure**

The more risk you take, the more you are unstoppable. You can go to any lengths despite the consequences. Risk takers eliminate that mental block called fear that hinders their journey.

6. **They set a High Standard**

Risk takers dream big. They want to get more after attaining a reward from some previous actions. With every risk that comes their way, they boost their will to venture further into unchartered territories

7. **They Learn all the way Through**

Risk takers don't harness knowledge. With every risk they take, they learn and know more about the type of risks they should take. Risk takers don't just dip themselves in any water. They analyse which chances are worth taking and then pursue them.

8. **They Change**

Risk takers are the most dynamic people on earth, and they attain more freedom and flexibility. They do not lack any ability as the process of taking risk helps them to either define a change or adapt to a situation. Risk takers are known to move with the tide and set the bar for even more significant changes. Granted, doing something different can mean utter discomfort and redirection of your thought process, yet getting out of that comfort zone is will always bear a mark along your journey to success and bring to you the life you have dreamt and wanted all along.

How Taking Risks to Attain Success

1. **The Key to Succeed is to Learn to Fail**

Many people may have a negative attitude towards the idea of failure, but actually, it can provide an essential tool for building our character. Failure makes us stronger and much more resilient. People who repeatedly fail generally develop persistence in the face of utmost difficulties. What does that tell us? Taking risks doesn't mean succeeding every time, and that is okay and acceptable. The process of taking risks may lead to the worst failures, but even that can make us a better person than before by increasing our capacity to recover quickly from such failures and difficulties.

2. **The One Thing Risk-Takers Have in Common is Overconfidence**

Failure might turn us into better people, but that doesn't make it any less difficult to take more and more risks. What propels risk takers to risk more? It is often seen that building confidence can help to overcome the fear of taking risks. Entrepreneurs go up against tremendous odds and face many failures to build a successful business. That indicates that taking significant risks without knowing the outcome helps in the path of success.

3. **Learning to Overcome Your Fears**

Confidence is a skill that can be learned. Through practice, we can develop better self-confidence and equip ourselves with the right skills to take risks. When we feel shy or afraid to venture into something, we can take action to build more confidence within ourselves. Instead of accepting oneself as a shy person, risk takers muster the courage to overcome the fears by facing them. In doing so, even doing something outside the comfort zone does not scare the person anymore.

4. **The Cycle of Success**

The take away is to take a risk to achieve a goal. It requires courage to face uncertainty. No matter what the outcome is, we learn and grow through the process and develop resilience and confidence.

CHAPTER TWENTY-TWO

WHY GAINING SKILL IS THE MOST SIGNIFICANT INVESTMENT IN TODAY'S WORLD

In today's world, there are many situations when any particular skill set has always benefited a person at a personal and professional need. What this means is that a person could still benefit from adding something to their free time. Not only can this help, but it also comes as handy in some situations where having a particular skill is required to deal with the situation. That is the reason why many of the companies to invest in their employees to learn any specific skill set which may help the employee and the organisation in the future.

Most employees and fresh out of college trainees always work in adding more and more skills in themselves because one, it may be useful for the company and two, it could also help in personal gains. Some companies even hire trainees and potential employees based on a variety of skills they possess.

Nowadays, even millennials are focused on increasing their own skill set. Because the time taken to learn a skill for themselves could always be an asset for any company. For Example, a graduate from a college could learn a particular language such as French or Spanish. This could help them get placements on an international level. Or taking another example, a web developer could learn any other programming language all by themselves or get a certified course through which they receive certification that they have completed the task of acquiring the particular skill. This could help in broadening the horizon of the opportunity of the person.

There are many benefits to learning a new skill. Some of them are:

- **For the sense of achievement:** A person could learn some skills as per their requirement. One of the elements could be for their passion, while others would learn a skill for their professional gain. Overall, if at all nothing, then the person could at least have pride in the fact that they learned something new which they could use in their future.

- **It makes a person learn faster:** Learning a new skill helps in boosting brain activity. It helps the brain process the further information which a person determines in their task of learning the new skill. Moreover, if the person is learning this skill in a limited period, they also train the brain to learn the thing or the skill faster without missing out the necessary details and lessons.

- **Connections are made in that particular skill areas:** If a person is learning a new skill, they will also be surrounded with people who are particularly well known for that specific skill and not only that, it could also help in connecting with the people who already have in-depth knowledge about the power. And not only could that it help in talking about the power which makes it relatable for a person to talk with each other. And it also helps in talking with a person who has more knowledge about the skill and could also help in adding information about the skill.

- **The person can be interesting to talk to:** Now, since a person knows about anything other than the regular topics, makes it easier for others to approach the persona and ask them about various topics. And it also boosts confidence. Moreover, it could also help other people know more about the skill, and it also makes the person appealing to talk to, where many different people are interested in initiating a conversation. And ultimately it also helps in improving the quality of life of a person's relations.

- **Helps in countering boredom:** Learning new things have proved that it fights boredom because it always helps in making a person involved in learning about the skill. Because doing the same things over and over again makes a person's life dull and monotonous. Whereas learning new things always is exciting.

- **Learning new skills improves adaptability:** Now, learning new skills also helps a person to adapt to various situations and also helps a person come out of a tight spot. Some skills make sure that the person knows everything about the choices and solution for any particular situation and not only that, it also helps them in adjusting to any change which their professional and personal life throws at them.

- **It helps in keeping Dementia at bay:** People who commit into learning a new skill are known to less likely develop signs of dementia as compared to people who do not take the effort into learning a new skill. It is said that learning more and more skills would help in creating more neural pathways through which a person's new neural impulses travel.

No matter what. Learning a new skill can be self-taught or can be acquired by undertaking a professional course. The most recommended course of action is to learn a skill which is being provided by an educational institution because they not only teach a person the basics of the skill set but also provide a written assurance or certificate.

CHAPTER TWENTY-THREE

STRATEGIES FOR PROFESSIONAL GROWTH AND SUCCESSFUL CAREER

Having a successful career comes with a lot of benefits and real profitable opportunities. As our society is governed by status and money, working your way up to the top improves your quality of life. A successful career offers you a feeling of security and accomplishment and to achieve it a gradual growth in professional experience is essential. Abiding by certain practices and habits has benefitted a large number of successful individuals around the world. Here are some of those useful practices listed below:

Strategies for Successful Career

1. Identify with Your Goals

Before considering a career path for yourself, identify yourself as a person. Know your innermost desires. Think about the goals you want to achieve and evaluate whether they are in synchronisation with your wishes. Adopt that as your career option only if your goals and desires coincide.

2. Build a Professional Resume

A resume is a list of your capabilities and previous experiences. A neat and impressive resume is pivotal to gain the attention of your employers. Opportunities are everywhere, and to grab those you should be ready with a perfect or impressive resume preferably designed by professionals.

3. Become Aware of Your Strengths

Self-awareness is an essential key to personal improvement. By being aware of your inner thoughts, strengths, desires, advantages, and disadvantages, you can adapt yourself to any situation. You will also get the leverage of choosing a career best suited to your traits and qualities.

4. Assume Full Responsibility for Your Life

Start assuming responsibility for your actions and do not blame anyone for your mistakes. Do not take things personally, and whenever something bad happens, you need to understand it. Even if you are not directly connected to the mishap, your previous actions and thoughts might have caused it.

5. Always Raise Your Standards

. Your standards influence your thoughts and behaviour. If your standards are high, you will always aim higher. People with high standards are mostly more successful than average people. Try to improve yourself bit by bit up until you've become the best version of yourself.

6. Brand Yourself

Branding is a very important factor nowadays. Big companies spend millions on improving their brand or image in the market. Professional employees should brand their names and services to improve them. Starting a blog, creating a professional social media profile, or simply providing excellent services is an effective way to build your brand.

7. Network

Networking helps to create opportunities and connections. When you meet new people, you get a chance to utilise their skills to your advantage. Creating profiles on LinkedIn, Twitter, and Facebook can help to boost your career.

Essential Professional Growth Strategies

1. Being hardworking and persistent

Hard work and persistence are indispensable for professional growth and success. When you give in your best in every project, your work performance enhances. Your effort and dedication will be most certainly noticed and will boost your career.

2. Setting achievable professional growth goals

Before advancing for any project, think about your specialties and the kind of projects you want to work on. Once you have a big picture, set small goals. That way, you will easily achieve short objectives and be motivated to persist till the end.

3. Knowing your strengths and weaknesses

One of the important strategies for professional growth is to be aware of your strengths and weaknesses. Evaluate your strong areas and take up only those projects that utilise your capabilities but do not exploit your vulnerabilities.

4. Developing leadership skills

Leadership is not a position but a process. Developing leadership skills opens up greater opportunities in the professional environment for you. Thinking outside the box, working on your communication skills and improving emotional intelligence are effective ways to develop leadership skills.

5. Following your principles

To have a truly fulfilling career adhere to your beliefs regarding task management, business communication, and work-life balance. When your policies align with your work ethics and environment, you can be satisfied with your job.

6. Striving for excellence

Striving for excellence ensures that you deliver quality work that meets the standards. This involves determining the areas in your work that are good and can be enhanced as the next step.

7. Being able to handle criticism

One of the prerequisites for professional growth is the ability to handle criticism. Negative feedback not only increases your resilience in the workplace but also helps to identify those areas where you are not putting your best. Taking blame in good stride ultimately enhances your range of abilities.

8. Tracking your progress

Working for betterment is of no use unless you can track your progress. No matter what task you do, map your progress after every week. This will show how much further you've gone to achieve your target and the shortcomings that prevent you from going also.

CHAPTER TWENTY-FOUR

SWOT ANALYSIS

SWOT analysis is a technique that helps a person or organisation to strategically plan and identify the strengths, weaknesses, opportunities, and threats that affect their business. This helps to clarify the objectives and identify the internal and external factors that boosters them.

SWOT is an acronym for the following four parameters:

- **Strengths**: aspects of the business that favours it.
- **Weaknesses**: characteristics of the business that are at a disadvantage.
- **Opportunities**: elements that can be exploited to advantage in business.
- **Threats**: elements that can harm a business or project.

Strategic fit highlights the degree to which the internal and external environment of a firm are compatible. SWOT analysis is important because they can throw light on future planning steps that will help achieve the objective. Decision makers should study the SWOTs and examine whether a target is attainable or not. If the objective is not attainable, they must opt for a different objective and repeat the process.

Internal Factors

SWOT analysis aims to identify the primary internal and external factors required to achieve an objective. SWOT analysis groups the information into two main categories:

1. Internal factors — the strengths and weaknesses of an organisation
2. External factors — the opportunities and threats presented by the external environment to the organisation

The analysis may classify strengths and weaknesses according to the different objectives of an organisation. What acts as strengths concerning one objective may pose as a weakness for another objective.

External Factors

The external factors include:

- Macroeconomic matters
- Technological change
- Legislation
- Sociocultural changes
- Changes in the marketplace.

The result is presented in the form of a matrix.

SWOT analysis is just a basic method of categorisation and has its disadvantages. For example, it tends to persuade its users to prepare lists rather than to analyse the real important factors

pivotal in achieving objectives. It uncritically presents the resulting lists, and without clearly prioritising them, for

Example, weak opportunities may appear to be balancing active threats. It is wise not to eliminate any candidate using SWOT entry too quickly. The importance of individual SWOT analysis reveals the value of strategies generated by it.

How to Do a SWOT Analysis

1. **Determine the objective:** Decide on the key idea of the project or strategy that is to be analysed and place it on the top of the page.
2. **Create a grid:** Draw a large square and divide it into four equally small squares.
3. **Label each box:** Write the word Strength inside the top left the box, Weaknesses inside the top right box, Opportunities inside the bottom left the box and Threats inside the bottom right box. These titles should be distinguished from one another by the use of varying text concerning both font colour and font size. Smart Draw offers various SWOT diagram templates for this purpose.
4. **Add strengths and weaknesses:** Jot down the factors that affect the project in the respective boxes. Components of a SWOT analysis can be qualitative, anecdotal, quantitative, or empirical. Factors are generally listed in a bullet or numbered form.
5. **Conclude:** Analyse the finished SWOT diagram. Make sure that the positive outcomes do not outweigh the negative. If they do, it may not be a good decision to carry out the objective. Make adjustments accordingly or else simply abandon the plan.

Tips for a Successful SWOT analysis

Before conducting a SWOT analysis, decide what you want to achieve with it and consider whether it is aptly suited for your needs. If you decide a SWOT analysis is the best tool, the following tips will help you to analyse it better: Keep your SWOT short and simple, but do not forget to include the important details.

1. When you finish your SWOT analysis, prioritise the results by listing them in descending order of the most significant factors to the least significant factors that affect your business.
2. Get multiple opinions and perspectives on your business for your SWOT analysis. Ask for input from the people involved in the business of those who help to run it, for example, employees, suppliers, customers, and partners.
3. Apply your SWOT analysis to a particular issue, such as a target you need to reach or a problem that requires a solution, rather than to the entire business. You can then conduct separate SWOT analyses and combine their results to get an overall output.
4. Look at where your business is now and think about the amount of growth you want to envisage in the future.
5. Consider your competitors' share in the market and realistically compare how much your business competes with them.
6. Think about the factors that are essential to the growth of your business, and the things only you or your business can offer to the market and customers, but your competitors cannot. This is called a competitive advantage, and it can be a turning point in the SWOT analysis.
7. Utilise the objective of the overall business or project in your SWOT analysis.

CHAPTER TWENTY-FIVE

Teammanagement is the ability of a person to coordinate with other individuals of the same workgroup to complete a project or task. It involves various aspects like teamwork, communication, the establishment of an objective and estimation of performance.

Characteristics of Healthy Team

1. Cohesive Leadership: A proper team requires a unidirectional thought process of the leader and teammates. Cohesive leadership will ensure that team leaders with strong communication skills, work with the team members as a unit, and there is no branching off.

2. Effective Communication: Every team follows a chain of command, and an effective channel of communication must be established to ensure smooth working of the team. This involves the timely exchange of information and updates at regular intervals. Effective communication reduces the delay of work and increases the flexibility of work between partners.

3. The common goal: No matter the variety of ideas that circulate in a team, the objective must remain the same. The team leader and the team members must share the same goal. If this is not the case, the ideas and energy expended by a member will go to waste without adequate utilisation.

4. Defined team roles and responsibilities: In a good team, every member has their own job description. This allows every member to work independently within the boundaries with no interference or confusion. Generally, the team leader divides the work amongst the members.

Who is a Team Leader?

A teamleader is a person who provides guidance, instruction, direction, and leadership *to* the team to achieve a coordinated and aligned result with his subordinates. The team leader monitors the progress of the team with respect to the contribution and achievement of each teammate and reports it to a manager. Team leaders utilise their expertise, influence, and creativity to form an effective team. Team leaders must possess enough skills to motivate their members to expend their energies in a way that helps the overall team to achieve their target. He must be a person capable enough to extract the best performance from people.

Leadership Styles in Team Management

1. Autocratic

Autocratic leaders make their own decisions without consulting the team members. Besides absolute authority, team leaders also demand compliance with their decision. Autocratic leaders use one-way communication, where they instruct team members and expect them to follow those without any question. This type of leadership style is advantageous in a way that decisions are made quickly in crucial times.

2. Democratic

Democratic leaders consult team members before making a decision. A two-way communication exists between team members and the leader as their opinions and inputs are also valued. Democratic team leaders must possess excellent communication skills to handle conflicting opinions of team members as well as convey his own opinion.

3. Laissez-Faire

Laissez-Faire is a leadership style where the team leader allows his or her members to perform the task independently. There is little or no exertion of authority. This style of leadership is best suited in product designing or advertising teams that require freedom and flexibility to generate a creative result. Although this suits team members well who cannot work under a controlled environment, there is always a chance of poor performance due to the nonexistence of any driving force.

4. Transactional

This type of leadership is the most commonly observed. The relationship between the team leader and team member is one of agreement. The team leader extracts the best performance from the members through rewards or punishments.

Leadership Methods of Team Management

1. Command and Control

Based on the concept of military management, Command and Control method is designed for autocratic leadership. The leader delivers instruction to the team and members refusing to follow it receive severe backlash. Command and Control establish the absolute authority of the leader. However, this method has several drawbacks. The constant threat of punishment lowers the confidence of team members and will do nothing to boost their performance. Also, in large organisations team leaders lack the huge amount of time required to instruct and monitor each and every member. This also prevents leaders from lending time to their core responsibilities.

2. Engage and Create

Command and Control have their own limitations and to combat that, an alternative strategy known as Engage and Create was developed. In this method, team members are encouraged to contribute to the team through discussions and participation. To increase productivity and accountability of every member and to build a strong sense of teamwork and unity, Engage and Create is essential.

3. Econ 101

Econ 101 method is based on the assumption that financial reward motivates all team members. This method uses the ideology of material gains instead of intrinsic motivation to extract the best performance. However, this method does not consider other forms of motivation, such as personal satisfaction and ambition to drive an employee. Moreover, as everyone is propelled by different factors, it may promote discontentment in the workplace as monetary rewards can never satisfy everyone. This compounds the negative effect through widespread demoralisation and loss of confidence.

CHAPTER TWENTY-SIX

WAYS TO GREET PEOPLE TO IMPROVE RELATIONSHIPS

The first step in starting a conversation is by greeting someone. What you say at the very first moment you see someone or speak on the telephone creates a lasting first impression. A proper greeting establishes the type of relationship that you can have with a person. When greeting someone, it is important that you use the appropriate level of formality for each situation. For example, business greetings are strictly formal, but if you can exude warmth even that greeting, it can ensure that your professional career flourishes a long way. Friendly greetings are generally informal, but through your address, you can communicate the degree of cosiness and informality the degree of cosiness and ease you want in a relationship.

Listed below are some strategies for making a good impression when you meet and greet people in person.

How to Greet People to Strengthen Relationships

1. **When you are greeting people in person for the first time**

To ensure that your first impression when you are meeting new people is positive, include a warm smile, an introduction with your first and last name, a welcoming comment, direct eye contact and a firm handshake as a part of your greeting. Repeat the person's name as often as you can. For example, "Hello, <person's name> pleased to meet you."

1. **When you meet people who do not tell you their name**

If the person does not reveal his name, use phrases like "I didn't catch your name." to get his name. After they respond, use the previously mentioned tactics to greet and converse with them.

3. **When someone introduces you and does not tell your name**

When you are introduced to a person or a group of people by a third person, and he or she forget to include your name, offer them a warm greeting as described in the first tip and make sure that you include your first and last name. This also proves that you are paying attention to the conversation.

4. **When you greet someone likely to have forgotten your name**

When you great people whom you have not met in a while, take the initiative to introduce yourself to them first hand. If you don't remember the person's name, introduce yourself by sharing your name and politely ask them to identify themselves using lines like, "Will you kindly remind me of your name?

5. **When you are not introduced**

When you meet a group of people, and you are not introduced to them, the general response is to introduce yourself to the right opportunity. This avoids an awkward situation and makes everyone feel more comfortable.

6. **When you meet with a group of people, you do not know**

Have you ever walked into a room full of strangers and did not know how to start a conversation? If this happens, be proactive and introduce yourself to every person in the room. This will project you as someone with confidence and will also make everyone feel more at ease.

7. **When you meet with a group of people you know**

When you get together or meet with a group of friends or business associates, immediately greet each person with a friendly greeting. In the case of friends, a casual and informal greeting works well too. If more and more new people join the group, be the first one to greet them and make them feel at ease. This strengthens bonds and solidifies human relationships too.

8. **When you meet with a group of people whom you don't know entirely**

When I find myself in a situation where you know some people in a group and not everyone, always greet the people you know and introduce myself to the people you have not yet met. Do not restrict your greetings to your known acquaintances only as this creates division and uncomfortable situation in the group. Once you mingle with everyone, the group is a cosy one.

9. **When you greet a receptionist**

Whether you are greeting the receptionist at any office, always introduce yourself with a smile and friendly greeting. In the case of a business environment, make sure that you always hand the receptionist your business card to go along with my verbal introduction.

10. **Practice, practice, practice**

If you follow the tips mentioned above, you can be assured of making a positive and great first impression. This can enhance your existing relationships as you will be viewed as someone who is friendly and confident and recognises the value of making people feel comfortable in any place or situation. The proper greeting is also a great way to boost your human resource skills and creates warmth in a relationship. Although these might feel uncomfortable at first, with regular practice, it becomes easy.

CHAPTER TWENTY-SEVEN

WHAT TO DO WHEN THE BRAIN GIVES UP?

There are various times in our life when we feel that we have had enough. Our brain convinces us that we have reached our limit of tolerance, and nothing can motivate us to keep on doing the task. Remember that your body and muscles are capable of a lot more than your brain tricks you to think. Giving up is nothing but a psychological state and is induced in times of severe physical and mental stress. Whenever you feel that things are beyond your capability, the brain slowly goes through various stages of mental disintegration until you lose your will to live. Therefore, it is very important to identify these stages of mental apathy and take proper measures to maintain your psychological balance.

Stages of the Brain Giving Up

1. **Social withdrawal**

Social withdrawal usually follows a psychological trauma and is considered as a way of coping. This is a very passive state and is characterised by withdrawal from social interaction, emotionlessness, indifference, and self-absorption.

2. Apathy

A person in the state of apathy exhibits seriously melancholic behaviour and lack of energy as if they no longer wish to preserve themselves. This state of mind is accompanied by not putting forth efforts towards much of anything.

3. **Aboulia**

The stage of Aboulia takes over when the mind essentially goes on a standby mode. It is as if the person has an empty mind or a consciousness devoid of rational thought or content. This is when a person not only severely lacks motivation but also has no emotional response to the point of refusing to speak. The sufferer becomes extremely withdrawn and has no desire or ability to help themselves or others.

4. **Psychic Akinesia**

The state of Psychic Akinesia is reached when a person is conscious but is in a state of such profound mental detachment that even extreme pain like from getting hit will initiate no response. A person in psychic akinesia can go to the point of not bathing and living in their excreta.

5. **Psychogenic Death**

This is the final stage and is called Psychogenic Death. In this stage, the person completely gives up. Someone who has reached this stage can lie in their excreta, and no warning, physical pain or pleading can make them want to live.

What To Do When The Brain Gives Up

1. Re-ignite the Motivational Fire

As things get increasingly difficult, you begin seeing things from a negative perspective. You may ponder on all things that have gone wrong, and you'll start questioning the need of those things. At this point, rekindle the urge that got you started in the first place like why you want to achieve that goal or opportunities you might be missing out if you give up. Visualize your target as a burning fire and keep adding incentives to fuel the need until you are sufficiently motivated.

2. Learn the Lesson and Use it to Your Advantage

Imagine how boring it would be if your life panned out exactly as it was supposed to be without any temporary defeat. The more you focus on finding the lessons in these difficult times, the shorter these times will be and of course, less challenging. Reframe the negative questions in your mind with a positive viewpoint. Although it may take time, eventually this negativity will invade your mind less and less often.

3. Plan Your Next Step Forward

The more you realize that you will keep moving forward no matter the consequence, you will need to plan how to do it. Determine how to take the first steps of the journey from utter difficulty to success. As soon as you have realized how to take those steps, embark on your journey. This will allow you to build the initial momentum very fast, and you can make progress to the point where you will start to forget that you even let the idea of giving up manipulate you.

4. Keep it Satisfyingly Simple

You may be chasing a goal that requires you to adapt to a lot of things and make a lot of changes. Trying to do everything at once can be psychologically, physiologically, emotionally, and spiritually taxing? Instead, break the whole process down into simple parts and make progress by completing one small target at a time. This way, you will be reprogramming your mind to achieve more and progress further. You will find that it has become your habit to achieve targets in the process of making progress. The exciting part of this venture is that you will find that your ultimate goal has snuck up on you and is just a stone's throw away. If you are feeling demotivated and your mind convinces you to give up, draw strength from the fact that all of your role models and idols went through the same ordeal during their turbulent times. You can draw strength from their methods until you pick yourself up, dust yourself, and continue on the path with much more vigor than before.

9 798885 556514

Printed by Libri Plureos GmbH in Hamburg,
Germany